## Rock Music Library

# Tupac Shakur

by Nathan Olson

Consultant: Meredith Rutledge
Assistant Curator
Rock and Roll Hall of Fame and Museum
Cleveland, Ohio

Capstone press

Mankato, Minnesota

Edge Books are published by Capstone Press
151 Good Counsel Drive, P.O. Box 669, Mankato, Minnesota 56002
www.capstonepress.com

*Library of Congress Cataloging-in-Publication Data*
Olson, Nathan.
    Tupac Shakur / by Nathan Olson.
    p. cm.—(Edge Books. Rock music library)
    Includes bibliographical references and index.
    ISBN 0-7368-2703-X (hardcover)
    1. Shakur, Tupac, 1971– 2. Rap musicians—United States—Biography—Juvenile
literature. [1. Shakur, Tupac, 1971– 2. Musicians. 3. Rap (Music) 4. African Americans—
Biography.] I. Title. II. Series.
ML3930.S48O57 2005
782.421649'092—dc22                                                          2003026405

Summary: Traces the life, career, and impact of rapper and actor Tupac Shakur.

**Editorial Credits**
Angela Kaelberer, editor; Jason Knudson, series designer; Molly Nei, book designer;
    Jo Miller, photo researcher; Scott Thoms, photo editor; Eric Kudalis, product
    planning editor

**Photo Credits**
AP/Wide World Photos/Frank Wiese, 6, 22; Jim Cooper, 11
Corbis/Mark Peterson, 17; Mitchell Gerber, 21
Corbis Sygma, 23, 29; Howard Jacqueline, cover
Getty Images Inc./Liaison/Evan Agostini, 24; Tim Mosenfelder, 5; Time Life
    Pictures/DMI, 9; Time Life Pictures/Kimberly Butler, 27
Globe Photos Inc./Anders Krusberg, 19
Michael Ochs Archives/Raymond Boyd, 15
WireImage/Tom Galella, 12

1 2 3 4 5 6 09 08 07 06 05 04

# Table of Contents

# CHAPTER 1

# Las Vegas Tragedy

On September 7, 1996, rapper and actor Tupac Shakur attended a boxing match in Las Vegas, Nevada. Tupac's friend Mike Tyson won the match in the first round. Marion "Suge" Knight and Tupac left the match in Suge's black BMW. They headed for Suge's dance club.

Suge stopped his car at a red light. A white Cadillac pulled up on the right. Someone in the Cadillac fired 13 bullets into Suge's car. Suge sped away, but it was too late. Four bullets had hit Tupac. He died in a hospital six days later. Tupac was only 25 years old.

## Learn about:

Shots in the dark

A life cut short

Tupac's impact

Tupac was only 25 years old when he died.

Tupac wanted to make life better for young African Americans.

## The Life of a Rap Star

Tupac's life is a story of struggle and success. His music brought him money, fame, and movie roles. It also brought him trouble. Some people wanted to ban Tupac's music. They thought his lyrics were cruel and violent.

Tupac always spoke his mind. He used his music to express his feelings. He wanted people to understand the hardships that many African Americans face.

Although his life was cut short, Tupac's music lives on today. Many rap and hip-hop artists are influenced by Tupac's songs, movies, and messages.

"He [Tupac] was a street journalist for those who were living the life he described in his work, saying the things other folks couldn't say."
—writer Eric Perkins

# CHAPTER 2

# Shining Serpent

In late 1970, Afeni Shakur was pregnant and in prison. She and 20 other people were charged with planning to bomb businesses in New York City. In May 1971, a jury found Afeni not guilty. She was released from prison. Afeni's time in prison had been stressful. She worried about her unborn baby's health.

On June 16, 1971, Afeni gave birth to a healthy boy. She named him Tupac Amaru. This name means "shining serpent." Tupac Amaru was the name of a powerful king of the Inca empire in South America. Afeni believed her son also would be a leader.

## Learn about:

Childhood

Early performances

Becoming a rapper

Tupac was named for a powerful South American king.

## Tough Times

Afeni was a single parent. Tupac's father, William Garland, was not a part of Tupac's life. In 1975, Afeni gave birth to a daughter, Sekyiwa. Sekyiwa's father didn't live with the family either.

Afeni did not have a steady job. The family lived in run-down apartments in New York City or stayed with friends.

Afeni wanted Tupac and Sekyiwa to have good educations. She made them go to school and do their homework. She hoped good educations would give them better lives.

"I had to teach my mother how to live in this world like it is today. She taught me how to live in that world that we have to strive for. And for that I'm forever grateful. She put heaven in my heart."
—Tupac Shakur, February 1996

Tupac's mother, Afeni, wanted her children to get good educations.

Tupac developed his talents at the Baltimore School of the Arts.

## Young Talent

Tupac loved to learn. He enjoyed reading and writing. He also liked to act and sing.

Afeni noticed her son's talents. She enrolled Tupac in the 127th Street Ensemble theater group. At 12, Tupac acted in the play *A Raisin in the Sun*.

When Tupac was 15, his family moved to Baltimore, Maryland. Tupac was accepted to the Baltimore School of the Arts. He studied ballet, poetry, music, and Shakespeare's plays. Tupac's talents made him one of the school's best students.

## Family Troubles

Tupac was happy at school, but miserable at home. Afeni started using crack cocaine. Soon, she was addicted to the drug. Tupac sometimes stayed with friends to avoid going home.

When Tupac was 17, Afeni moved the family to Marin City, California. Tupac didn't want to live with his mother. He stayed with a family friend in Marin City.

## Tupac's Big Break

Tupac found new problems in California. Other kids teased him because he liked poetry and drama. Tupac dropped out of school and started selling illegal drugs to make money.

Tupac's friends helped him change his life. They told him he was too talented to waste his life selling drugs. Tupac began rapping in their group, the One Nation Emcees. Soon after, Tupac met Leila Steinberg. She ran a program that brought artists into schools. Leila asked Tupac to work with her. She also invited him to live with her and her family.

Leila introduced Tupac to the members of Digital Underground (D.U.). D.U. was a popular rap and hip-hop group. They hired Tupac to be a background rapper and dancer. In 1990, Tupac went on tour with D.U. In his spare time, he wrote rap songs. He was eager to record his own CD.

*In 1990, Tupac (left) began performing with Digital Underground.*

# CHAPTER 3

# Rapper and Movie Star

In 1991, Tupac released his first solo rap CD, *2Pacalypse Now*. He used the name 2Pac. Tupac rapped about racism and violence in African American communities. The CD's success made Tupac a star.

Tupac also became a movie star. He got a part in the movie *Juice*.

Tupac continued to make music and movies in the early 1990s. In 1993, Tupac released his second solo CD. He starred with Janet Jackson in the movie *Poetic Justice*. In 1994, Tupac acted in the movie *Above the Rim*.

## Learn about:

Early success

First brush with death

Tupac's comeback

In 1994, Tupac played the part of Birdie in the movie *Above the Rim*.

## Trouble Ahead

Many of Tupac's songs had violent lyrics. Some of these lyrics reflected events in Tupac's life. In 1993, Tupac was involved in a shootout with police in Atlanta, Georgia. He was arrested twice for assault. While filming *Above the Rim*, Tupac was arrested again. He faced a 25-year prison term on sexual assault charges. Tupac claimed he was innocent.

Tupac's case went to trial in November 1994. On the last day of the trial, he went to Quad Studios in New York City to record a song. Inside the studio, two men robbed Tupac and shot him five times.

Tupac survived the attack and went to court the next day in a wheelchair. The court found Tupac guilty of the sexual assault charges. The judge sentenced him to a prison term of 18 months to four and one-half years.

"I think that honestly, Tupac was the greatest songwriter that ever lived. He made it seem so easy."

—*rap star Eminem*

On December 1, 1994, Tupac came to court in a wheelchair.

## Prison Life

In February 1995, Tupac began serving his prison term. Tupac's third CD, *Me Against the World*, was released while he was in prison. Right after its release, the CD went to number one on the music charts.

Tupac could not enjoy his success. He missed his career. Tupac was also angry about being robbed and shot. He thought the robbery was set up by rappers Sean "P. Diddy" Combs and Christopher "Biggie Smalls" Wallace. Wallace rapped as the Notorious B.I.G.

Tupac thought about changing his life. He decided to make smarter choices. He also planned to start a group to help kids stay out of trouble.

"What I want to do is form a society in which we can raise ourselves ... and then you grow up, then it's your turn to be a father figure to another young brother. That's where I want to start."
—Tupac Shakur, June 1996

Tupac's rivals included Biggie Smalls (center) and P. Diddy (right). Lil' Kim is at left.

## A Second Chance

Tupac's friends came to see him in prison. Suge Knight visited most often. Suge was the head of Death Row Records. Suge wanted to sign Tupac to a recording contract. Friends warned Tupac that Suge was involved in a gang. Tupac wasn't sure about the deal, but he needed money. In October 1995, Tupac signed a contract with Death Row Records.

**Suge Knight (right) was one of Tupac's closest friends.**

Soon after, Tupac's lawyers appealed
his prison sentence. Tupac was released
from prison. He started working on new
projects. Tupac acted in the movies *Bullet,
Gridlock'd*, and *Gang Related*. He also released
rap music's first double CD, *All Eyez on Me*.
The CD sold more than 5 million copies.

Tupac attended the MTV Video Music Awards just three days before he was shot.

# Too Young to Die

Rap music began on the East Coast. Many early rappers lived in New York City or Philadelphia. Later, rap spread to the West Coast. West Coast rap was centered in Los Angeles and Oakland, California.

Although Tupac was born in New York, he said he was a West Coast rapper. In his songs, he taunted East Coast rappers like P. Diddy and Biggie Smalls. In turn, P. Diddy and Smalls taunted Tupac. Some people thought the taunts would lead to violence.

Tupac's record deal with Suge also put him at risk. Suge was powerful in the music business, but he had many enemies. Tupac understood the risks. He remained loyal to Suge.

On September 7, 1996, Tupac was in Las Vegas. He watched Mike Tyson's boxing match with Suge and other friends. Later that night, Tupac was shot. He died six days later.

# CHAPTER 4

# Rap's Loss

Tupac's death shocked the music world. Fans gathered to remember him. They lit candles and left flowers in his honor.

Tupac's death raised many questions. Some people think Suge Knight's enemies killed Tupac. Other people think the killers were friends of the East Coast rappers. Biggie Smalls was shot and killed six months after Tupac's death. Some people believe Smalls' murder was revenge for Tupac's death. Tupac's murder remains unsolved.

## Learn about:

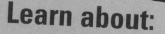

An unsolved killing

Music lives on

Tupac's poetry

After his death, Tupac's fans created memorials in his honor.

## The Legend Lives On

Tupac's memory stays alive through his music and movies. Five solo CDs and two movies were released after Tupac's death. In 1997, Tupac received the American Music Award for Favorite Rap/Hip-Hop artist.

People remember Tupac in other ways. Movies, books, and plays have been produced about Tupac's life. Tupac's mother started the Tupac Amaru Shakur Foundation in Georgia. The group helps young people who are interested in the performing arts.

In his short life, Tupac influenced the music world. He helped make rap music more popular. He also made people aware of the difficulties many African Americans face. His music and movies made him a rap legend.

# Tupac's Poetry

After Tupac died, his family and friends put together a book of his poems. They called the book *The Rose That Grew from Concrete.* The title comes from a poem that Tupac wrote about his struggles growing up.

The book contains poems Tupac wrote throughout his life. One of the poems is called "In the Event of My Demise." In the poem, Tupac wrote about his feeling that he would die young.

# Glossary

**appeal** (uh-PEEL)—to ask for a decision made by a court of law to be changed

**assault** (ah-SAWLT)—a violent attack on another person

**crack cocaine** (KRAK koh-KAYN)—a powerful, dangerous illegal drug

**influence** (IN-floo-uhnss)—to have an effect on someone or something

**lyrics** (LIHR-iks)—the words of a song

**serpent** (SUR-puhnt)—a snake

**taunt** (TAWNT)—to use words to try to make someone angry

# Read More

**Armentrout, David, and Patricia Armentrout.** *Rap.*
Sounds of Music. Vero Beach, Fla.: Rourke, 1999.

**Forkos, Heather.** *Tupac Shakur.* They Died Too Young.
Philadelphia: Chelsea House, 2001.

**Lommel, Cookie.** *The History of Rap Music.*
African-American Achiever. Philadelphia: Chelsea
House, 2001.

# Internet Sites

FactHound offers a safe, fun way to
find Internet sites related to this book.
All of the sites on FactHound have
been researched by our staff.

Here's how:
1. Visit *www.facthound.com*
2. Type in this special code **073682703X** for age-appropriate
   sites. Or enter a search word related to this book for a
   more general search.
3. Click on the **Fetch It** button.

FactHound will fetch the best sites for you!

# Index